Johann Christoph
PEPUSCH

(1667 – 1752)

Sonata IV for Flute and Basso continuo
F Major / Fa majeur / F-Dur

Edited by
Mechthild Winter and Thomas Reimann

DOWANI International

Preface

Thomas Reimann, freelance flautist and lecturer at the Hochschule für Musik und Theater Leipzig, has performed this sonata for flute and basso continuo in F Major by Johann Christoph Pepusch, and has arranged the flute part. The composer, who was born in Berlin, first lived in the Netherlands and later settled in London, where he became a co-founder of the Academy of Ancient Music. Pepusch was not only a popular composer, but was also one of the first historic researchers of early music. Our edition enables you to work your way through this sonata systematically and in three differing tempi with a professional accompaniment.

The CD opens with the concert version of each movement (flute and basso continuo). After tuning your instrument (Track 1), the musical work can begin. Your first practice session should be at slow tempo. If your stereo system is equipped with a balance control, you can place either the flute or the harpsichord accompaniment in the foreground by adjusting the control. The flute always remains softly audible in the background as a guide. In the middle position, both instruments can be heard at the same volume. If you do not have a balance control, you can listen to the solo part on one loudspeaker and the harpsichord part on the other. After having learnt this piece at a slow tempo, you can proceed by practising the second and fourth movements at a moderate tempo, too. We have decided against offering moderate tempo versions of the first and third movements, since the originals of both are relatively slow. Now you can play the piece with accompaniment at the original tempo. At the me-

dium and original tempos, the continuo accompaniment can be heard on both channels (without flute) in stereo quality. All of the versions were recorded live. The names of the musicians are listed on the last page of this volume; further information can be found in the Internet at www.dowani.com.

A few slurs have been added to the solo part. However, the musician him- or herself can and should add his or her own embellishments (trills, inverted mordents, mordents etc.). This of course also applies to the realisation of the basso continuo.

The realisation of the basso continuo offered here is limited to one possible basic realisation of the figured bass with a few ideas on rhythm and dynamics (reduction of number of parts to two or three parts). It was not possible to print out the many various possibilities offered by the harpsichord, such as a full accompaniment, ornamentation, or arpeggio accompaniment, since they are largely dependent on the technical skill and taste of the accompanist, and also have to suit the soloist's interpretation. Accompanists who are familiar with playing basso continuo will be able to play from the figured bass part.

We wish you lots of fun playing from our *DOWANI 3 Tempi Play Along* editions and hope that your musicality and diligence will enable you to play the concert version as soon as possible. Our goal is to provide the essential conditions you need for effective practicing through motivation, enjoyment and fun.

Your DOWANI Team

Avant-propos

Thomas Reimann, flûtiste en free-lance et professeur à l'École Supérieure de Musique et Théâtre de Leipzig, a enregistré la présente Sonate pour flûte et basse continue en Fa majeur de Johann Christoph Pepusch et a réglé la partie de flûte. Né à Berlin, le compositeur s'installa d'abord aux Pays-Bas pour s'établir ensuite à Londres où il fut co-fondateur de l'"Academy of Ancient Music". Pepusch n'était non seulement un compositeur apprécié, il compte aussi parmi les premiers musicologues. Notre édition vous permet d'étudier la sonate de manière systématique dans trois tempos différents avec un accompagnement professionnel.

Le CD vous permettra d'entendre d'abord la version de concert de chaque mouvement (flûte et basse continue). Après avoir accordé votre instrument (plage n° 1), vous pourrez commencer le travail musical. Votre premier contact avec le morceau devrait se faire à un tempo lent. Si

votre chaîne hi-fi dispose d'un réglage de balance, vous pouvez l'utiliser pour mettre au premier plan soit la flûte, soit l'accompagnement de clavecin. La flûte restera cependant toujours très doucement à l'arrière-plan comme point de repère. En équilibrant la balance, vous entendrez les deux instruments à volume égal. Si vous ne disposez pas de réglage de balance, vous entendrez l'instrument soliste sur un des haut-parleurs et le clavecin sur l'autre. Après avoir étudié le morceau dans le tempo lent, vous pouvez étudier les 2e et 4e mouvements aussi dans un tempo moyen. Concernant les 1er et 3e mouvements, nous avons renoncé au tempo moyen, puisque leurs tempos originaux sont déjà relativement lents. Vous pourrez ensuite jouer le tempo original. Dans ces deux tempos vous entendrez l'accompagnement de la basse continue sur les deux canaux en stéréo (sans la partie de flûte). Toutes les versions ont été enregistrées en direct. Vous trouverez les noms des artistes qui ont participé aux enregistrements sur la dernière page de cette édition ; pour obtenir plus de renseignements, veuillez consulter notre site Internet : www.dowani.com.

Quelques liaisons ont été ajoutées dans la partie du soliste. L'exécutant est bien entendu invité à ajouter ses propres phrasés et ornements (tremblements, battements, mordants etc.). Cela concerne également la réalisation de la basse continue.

Notre édition se borne à une réalisation basique de la basse continue, comportant quelques suggestions concernant le rythme et la dynamique (réduction du nombre des voix à deux ou trois). Les nombreuses possibilités de réalisation, comme le jeu à pleine main, les ornements ou encore les arpèges, ne peuvent pas être présentées dans ce cadre puisqu'elles dépendent essentiellement du savoir-faire et du goût de l'accompagnateur et doivent aussi être en corrélation avec l'interprétation du soliste. Les accompagnateurs familiers avec la basse continue peuvent directement utiliser la partie de basse chiffrée.

Nous vous souhaitons beaucoup de plaisir à faire de la musique avec la collection *DOWANI 3 Tempi Play Along* et nous espérons que votre musicalité et votre application vous amèneront aussi rapidement que possible à la version de concert. Notre but est de vous offrir les bases nécessaires pour un travail efficace par la motivation et le plaisir.

Les Éditions DOWANI

Vorwort

Thomas Reimann, freischaffender Flötist und Dozent an der Hochschule für Musik und Theater Leipzig, hat die vorliegende Sonate für Flöte und Basso continuo in F-Dur von Johann Christoph Pepusch eingespielt und die Flötenstimme eingerichtet. Der in Berlin geborene Komponist ging zunächst in die Niederlande und etablierte sich später in London, wo er Mitbegründer der „Academy of Ancient Music" wurde. Pepusch war nicht nur ein beliebter Komponist, sondern gehörte auch zu den ersten historischen Musikforschern. Unsere Ausgabe ermöglicht es Ihnen, die vorliegende Sonate systematisch und in drei verschiedenen Tempi mit professioneller Begleitung zu erarbeiten.

Auf der CD können Sie zuerst die Konzertversion (Flöte und Basso continuo) eines jeden Satzes anhören. Nach dem Stimmen Ihres Instrumentes (Track 1) kann die musikalische Arbeit beginnen. Ihr erster Übe-Kontakt mit dem Stück sollte im langsamen Tempo stattfinden. Wenn Ihre Stereoanlage über einen Balance-Regler verfügt, können Sie durch Drehen des Reglers entweder die Flöte oder die Cembalobegleitung stufenlos in den Vordergrund blenden. Die Flöte bleibt jedoch immer – wenn auch sehr leise – hörbar. In der Mittelposition erklingen beide Instrumente gleich laut. Falls Sie keinen Balance-Regler haben, hören Sie das Soloinstrument auf dem einen Lautsprecher, das Cembalo auf dem anderen. Nachdem Sie das Stück im langsamen Tempo einstudiert haben, können Sie den zweiten und vierten Satz auch im mittleren Tempo üben. Beim ersten und dritten Satz haben wir auf das mittlere Tempo verzichtet, da sie im Original schon relativ langsam sind. Anschließend können Sie sich im Originaltempo begleiten lassen. Die Basso-continuo-Begleitung erklingt im mittleren und originalen Tempo auf beiden Kanälen (ohne Flöte) in Stereo-Qualität. Alle eingespielten Versionen wurden live aufgenommen. Die Namen der Künstler finden Sie auf der letzten Seite dieser Ausgabe; ausführlichere Informationen können Sie im Internet unter www.dowani.com nachlesen.

In der Solostimme wurden einige Bindungen hinzugefügt. Der Spieler oder die Spielerin darf und soll jedoch gerne auch eigene Ergänzungen (Triller, Mordente, Praller usw.) hinzufügen. Dies gilt natürlich ebenso für die Ausführung des Generalbasses.

Die Aussetzung des Generalbasses beschränkt sich auf eine mögliche grundlegende Realisierung des bezifferten Basses mit einigen Ideen zu Rhythmus und Dynamik (Reduzierung der Stimmenanzahl auf drei oder zwei Stimmen). Die vielfältigen Gestaltungsmöglichkeiten am Cembalo wie vollstimmiges Spiel, Verzierungen oder Arpeggiogestaltung sind in diesem Rahmen nicht darstellbar, denn sie obliegen dem Können und musikalischen Geschmack des Begleiters und müssen mit der Interpretation des Solisten korrespondieren. Begleiter, die mit dem Generalbassspiel vertraut sind, können aus der bezifferten Bassstimme spielen.

Wir wünschen Ihnen viel Spaß beim Musizieren mit unseren *DOWANI 3 Tempi Play Along*-Ausgaben und hoffen, dass Ihre Musikalität und Ihr Fleiß Sie möglichst bald bis zur Konzertversion führen werden. Unser Ziel ist es, Ihnen durch Motivation, Freude und Spaß die notwendigen Voraussetzungen für effektives Üben zu schaffen.

Ihr DOWANI Team

Sonata IV

for Flute and Basso continuo
F Major / Fa majeur / F-Dur

J. Ch. Pepusch (1667 – 1752)
Continuo Realization: M. Winter

DOW 5518

Johann Christoph
PEPUSCH

(1667 – 1752)

Sonata IV for Flute and Basso continuo
F Major / Fa majeur / F-Dur

Flute / Flûte traversière / Querflöte

DOWANI International

Flute

Sonata IV

for Flute and Basso continuo
F Major / Fa majeur / F-Dur

I ②

J. Ch. Pepusch (1667 – 1752)
Edited by T. Reimann

II ③

DOW 5518

11

9 | 15 | 21

15

18

22

26

29

10 | 22

III 4

Adagio

7

11 | 23

14

22

4

IV ⑤

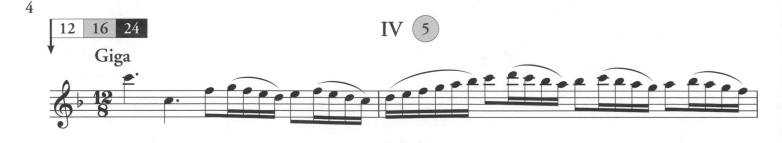

Giga

Johann Christoph
PEPUSCH

(1667 – 1752)

Sonata IV for Flute and Basso continuo
F Major / Fa majeur / F-Dur

Basso continuo / Basse continue / Generalbass

DOWANI International

Basso continuo

Sonata IV

for Flute and Basso continuo
F Major / Fa majeur / F-Dur

I

J. Ch. Pepusch (1667 – 1752)

DOW 5518

3

II

Allegro

4

III

Adagio

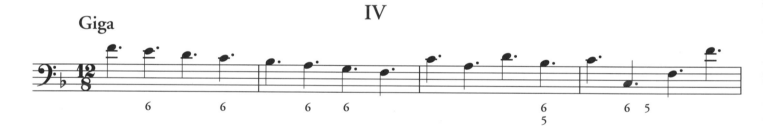

IV

Giga

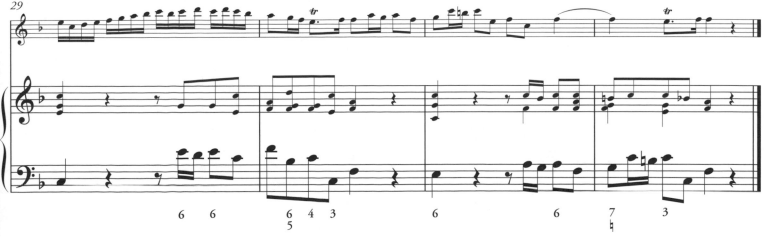

8

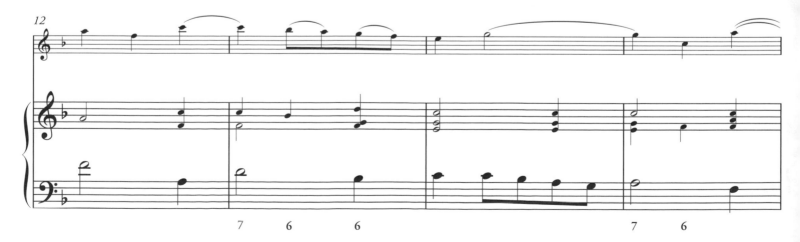

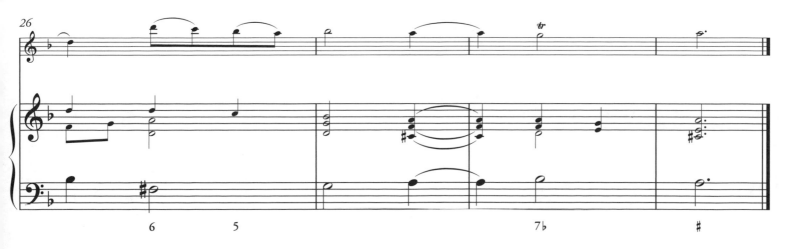

10

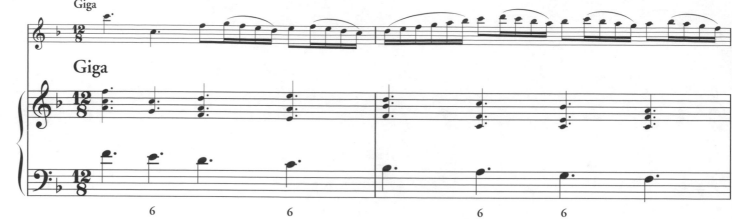

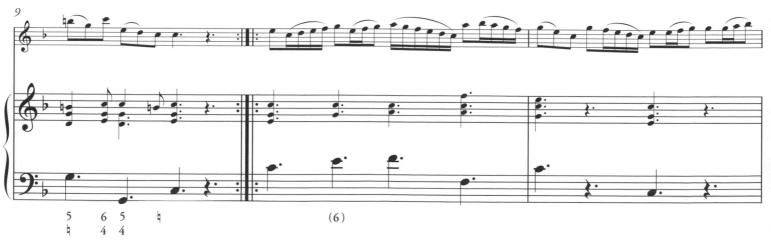

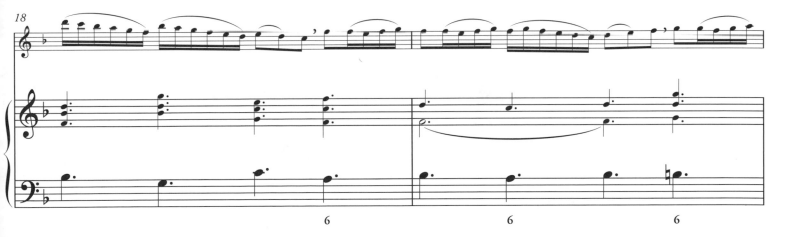

ENGLISH

DOWANI CD:
- Track No. 1
- Track numbers in circles
- Track numbers in squares

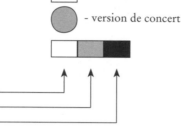

| 1 | - tuning notes |

- concert version

- slow Play Along Tempo
- intermediate Play Along Tempo
- original Play Along Tempo

- Additional tracks for longer movements or pieces
- **Concert version:** flute and basso continuo
- **Slow tempo:** channel 1: flute solo; channel 2: harpsichord accompaniment; middle position: both channels at the same volume
- **Intermediate tempo:** basso continuo only
- **Original tempo:** basso continuo only

Please note that the recorded version of the harpsichord accompaniment ma
differ slightly from the sheet music. This is due to the spontaneous characte
of live music making and the artistic freedom of the musicians. The original
sheet music for the solo part is, of course, not affected.

FRANÇAIS

DOWANI CD :
- Plage N° 1
- N° de plage dans un cercle
- N° de plage dans un rectangle

| 1 | - diapason |

- version de concert

- tempo lent play along
- tempo moyen play along
- tempo original play along

- Plages supplémentaires pour mouvements ou morceaux longs
- **Version de concert :** flûte et basse continue
- **Tempo lent :** 1er canal : flûte solo ; 2nd canal : accompagnement de clavecin ; au milieu : les deux canaux au même volume
- **Tempo moyen :** seulement l'accompagnement de la basse continue
- **Tempo original :** seulement l'accompagnement de la basse continue

L'enregistrement de l'accompagnement de clavecin peut présenter quelques
différences mineures par rapport au texte de la partition. Ceci est du à la liberté
artistique des musiciens et résulte d'un jeu spontané et vivant, mais n'affecte, bi
entendu, d'aucune manière la partie soliste.

DEUTSCH

DOWANI CD:
- Track Nr. 1
- Trackangabe im Kreis
- Trackangabe im Rechteck

| 1 | - Stimmtöne |

- Konzertversion

- langsames Play Along Tempo
- mittleres Play Along Tempo
- originales Play Along Tempo

- Zusätzliche Tracks bei längeren Sätzen oder Stücken
- **Konzertversion:** Flöte und Basso continuo
- **Langsames Tempo:** 1. Kanal: Flöte solo; 2. Kanal: Cembalobegleitung; Mitte: beide Kanäle in gleicher Lautstärke
- **Mittleres Tempo:** nur Basso continuo
- **Originaltempo:** nur Basso continuo

Die Cembalobegleitung auf der CD-Aufnahme kann gegenüber dem
Notentext kleine Abweichungen aufweisen. Dies geht in der Regel auf die
künstlerische Freiheit der Musiker und auf spontanes, lebendiges Musiziere
zurück. Die Solostimme bleibt davon selbstverständlich unangetastet.

DOWANI - 3 Tempi Play Along is published by:
DOWANI International
A division of De Haske (International) AG
Postfach 60, CH-6332 Hagendorn
Switzerland
Phone: +41-(0)41-785 82 50 / Fax: +41-(0)41-785 82 58
Email: info@dowani.com
www.dowani.com

Recording & Digital Mastering: Wachtmann Musikproduktion, Germany
Music Notation: Notensatz Thomas Metzinger, Germany
Design: Andreas Haselwanter, Austria
Printed by: Zrinski d.d., Croatia
Made in Switzerland

Concert Versio
Thomas Reimann, Flut
Mechthild Winter, Harpsichor
Isolde Winter, Baroque Cell

3 Tempi Accompanimen
Slow
Mechthild Winter, Harpsichor

Intermediate
Mechthild Winter, Harpsichor
Isolde Winter, Baroque Cell

Original
Mechthild Winter, Harpsichor
Isolde Winter, Baroque Cell